A Regency Lexicon
for
Readers and Writers

CAROL GOSS

Copyright © 2017 Carol Goss

All rights reserved. By payment of the required fees, you have been granted the non-exclusive, non-transferable right to read this book. No part of this text may be reproduced, transmitted, decompiled, reverse engineered, or stored in or introduced into any information storage and retrieval system, in any form or by any means, whether electronic or mechanical, now known or hereinafter invented, without the express written permission of author, Carol Goss.

ISBN: 1544935846
ISBN-13: 978-1544935843

DEDICATION

This book is dedicated
to my mother.

Mary Lucile Goss Mannino

She loved books and history and taught me
to read before I even started school.

Also, my thanks to author, R. C. Matthews
for her help in publishing this eBook.
I couldn't have done it without your support.

CONTENTS

Introduction	i
A	1
B	4
C	10
D	18
E	22
F	23
G	26
H	29
I	32
J	33
L	34
M	36
N	42
O	44
P	45
Q	51
R	51
S	55
T	59
U	61
V	61
W	62
Y	64

About the Author

INTRODUCTION

I hope you'll find this lexicon helpful and that it will increase your enjoyment of the many wonderful Regency novels available in your bookstores, libraries, and online.

Not all these words were used by the ton (See the definition of that word in the lexicon.) during the Regency. Some were used by other classes. In that case, the fact is indicated by the word **cant**, meaning lower class or criminal slang, or by reference to Cockney or other special groups who used the word. Otherwise, the slang listed was used by the ton at times, though probably more by the freewheeling types like the rakes and rogues than by more genteel folk.

You will also notice there are some French words or phrases in this glossary. Remember, the upper classes of the Regency were supposed to be familiar with the French language and, in most cases, actually were. Also, many aspects of French culture permeated English society even though the English, for a great deal of the period, were fighting the French in the Napoleonic Wars. If a French word was in regular use in Regency English, I've listed it in this glossary. If you wish to have a REGENCY GLOSSARY OF FOREIGN WORDS (mostly French), you'll also find one of those on my website at www.carolgoss.com for your use.

If anyone has a better or more complete definition of an entry, thinks I am wrong about the meaning of a word, or questions whether it was used during any part of the Regency period or at least has been used by writers of Regency novels, please contact me with your concerns. If there are errors, I want to correct them so this lexicon will be truly useful to readers and writers of all

types of novels set in our favorite period. Also, if there are any words you feel should be listed but aren't, do let me know. I will try to add them from time to time though no lexicon can be totally complete. Again, you can contact me at www.carolgoss.com

However, if you wish to link my foreign word online glossary to your website or to pass it on to any person or group in any fashion, I grant permission to do so, as long as you include the following statement at the beginning of the online glossary when you link or pass it on in any form:

"This glossary was compiled by and is the property of the romance author, Carol Goss, and is available on her website at www.carolgoss.com. It is reproduced here with her permission."

I hope this lexicon and the foreign word glossary at my website make your reading more enlightening and much more fun.

ENJOY!

A REGENCY LEXICON FOR READERS AND WRITERS

A

abigail – a lady's maid.

ablutions – the act of washing or cleansing one's face or body.

accomplishments – Since most upper class women were not expected to be educated in our sense of the word, an "accomplished" young lady was expected to have been trained in such talents such as painting watercolors, speaking French, playing the pianoforte (as the instrument was called then), dancing, embroidery as well as other forms of decorative needlework rather than actually being educated as young men of the upper class usually were.

accoucheur – an obstetrician. These were male physicians who specialized in childbirth, and it was thought more prestigious to have one attend the mother at the birth of a child than to have a general physician or midwife do it. These doctors were the first to use forceps to remove babies from the womb when problems arose.

addlepated – muddled; confused.

affair of honor – (see duel below).

ague – most commonly, a fever caused by malaria during which the patient alternately sweats and then becomes chilled, a condition that repeats and repeats or used to describe any chill with any cause such as catching cold or the flu or any spell of shivering or shaking.

all the crack – very fashionable.

Almack's – was the only club in London catering to members of both sexes which was most unusual in England as most clubs were for men only. It opened for the first time in December, 1769 and was controlled by a select group of six or seven women who ruled society. However, the patronesses, (see patroness below.) as they were called, of 1814 and later are the ones most written about in romance novels. They were Lady Castlereagh, Lady Sarah Jersey (often referred to as Sally), Lady Cowper, Lady Sefton, Mrs. Burrel, later to become Lady Gwydr in 1816, the Countess de Lieven who was the wife of the Russian ambassador, and Princess Esterhazy who was the wife of the Austrian ambassador. The patronesses had always been the ones who decided who could or could not attend the weekly dances held during the Season (see Season below). To their credit, the ladies did not make their choices simply on wealth or on social rank. Not be granted a voucher to Almack's did not necessarily make you a social outcast. However, if you'd been granted a voucher and then it was revoked, that did ruin your reputation for it meant the patronesses had found you guilty of a serious transgression of the rules of society, at least by their standards. As an example, the waltz was not considered a dance for respectable people until it was introduced at Almack's in 1814, supposedly by Lady Jersey.

Almack's also had two serious purposes for the upper classes, especially as the reign of George III neared its end. The first was to choose members for their high social standing and/or connections as well as their high society manners thus excluding the up-and-coming tradesmen developing great wealth as the Industrial Age began to make itself felt in Britain. The second was to provide the come-out ball for those young ladies accepted by the patronesses as worthy of a come-out at Almack's. Those debutantes could then search for a husband from among the most socially eligible bachelors in London. In other words, the come-out ball at Almack's was the most important marriage mart of the year among the ton (see marriage mart below). Besides dancing, there was also gambling at Almack's, and food was served, though it seems to have been of the tea party type. That no alcoholic drinks were served there made it not so attractive to the male members of society as the Regency was a period of heavy drinking, especially among men.

almshouse – for indigent people, privately run charities both secular and religious, not supported by the government.

alt – usually used as "in alt" – ecstatic, high, overjoyed, or in heaven.

amanuensis – a companion or employee who writes down what another says or who makes copies of what that person has written.

Angelo's Fencing Academy – located on Bond Street, it was where the men of the British aristocracy took exercise and practiced the art of fencing. It was a fashionable place for men to meet, a sort of private club and gymnasium, and many famous fencers put on exhibitions there. It was also a place for aristocrats to practice their marksmanship as it had a shooting range, and for a change of pace, they could go right next door to practice their boxing skills at Gentleman Jackson's (see Gentleman Jackson below).

antidote – an unattractive woman; a hatchet-faced ape leader.

ape leader – a derogatory word for a spinster or old maid.

apoplexy – Regency word for an attack that a person often died from. It was either a stroke or a heart attack, but there was simply no way at that time to tell which.

apothecary – what Americans would call a druggist and the English of today would call a chemist. He filled prescriptions for doctors and also often specialized in herbal remedies. Those who did not work with doctors were often considered quacks.

approbation – as a noun: a favorable opinion; approval/ as a verb: to formally and authoritatively approve or give sanction to something another has done or will do.

argle-bargle – (Cant) argument.

aristos – somewhat derogatory term for French aristocrats in exile in England during the French Revolution.

article – a wench; a pretty girl, often referred to as a "prime article."

articled – adjective applied to a clerk (see clerk below). who was bound by the terms of apprenticeship, covenant or other stipulation to a barrister or solicitor. It was like being under contract.

askance – with suspicion or disapproval **or** to one side; sideways.

assembly room – most towns of any size had one for public use, mostly dances where young people could be introduced to each other since it was improper for them to introduce themselves. Even Almack's was one (see Almack's above).

Astley's Amphitheatre – (see Royal Amphitheatre below).

au tartare – a French phrase for raw steak but used by the English during the Regency to mean raw, as in raw scandal or raw information, that which is especially destructive or awful or not proven.

B

bacon-brained – foolish, stupid. This is probably a Heyerism (see Heyerism below).

bagatelle – game played on a board that has holes at one end. The object is to strike balls with a cue and send them into the holes. The game seems to be an early form of pinball.

Children could play this game also.

baggage – familiar term for women or children.

baize – soft, and usually green, woolen or cotton fabric resembling felt used chiefly to top billiard tables.

bamming – tricking or fooling or telling tall tales.

Banbury Tale – used to describe a roundabout, nonsensical, or unbelievable story or tale.

bank draft – written for the same purpose a check is today, it was a written order from one person or bank to another, requiring the payment of a stated amount of money to the person, bank or merchant listed in the bank draft.

banns – a notice of an upcoming marriage that had to be read out on three Sundays in a row in the couple's parish church. If no one objected to the match during this period, the marriage proceeded. The marriage had to take place in whichever church the banns had been read and, if the two people lived in two different parishes, the banns had to be read in both. The marriage could take place in either parish in that case, but only between the hours of 8 am and noon. This then was a public wedding rather than a private one. (For more information on Regency marriage, see marriage and special license below.)

barking irons – pistols.

barouche – a large carriage with a driver's seat in front. It had two double passenger seats and was pulled by four horses. There was a folding hood that could be raised to cover two of the passengers.

barrister – the only lawyer allowed to argue cases in a court of law (see solicitor below). He did not handle contracts, wills or such, but only court cases. This is still true in English law.

barrow boy or girl – one who sells wares from a barrow on the street; a costermonger. (See costermonger below for date of change of the word.)

Bartholomew baby – a person dressed in a gaudy manner, like the dolls sold at Bartholomew Fair (a 2-week festival celebrating the Feast of St. Bartholomew).

batman – an orderly in the army assigned to a military officer to serve as his personal servant or valet.

Bath chair – a wheelchair. (Its name comes from its use for invalids at the spa city of Bath.)

battledore – an earlier form of badminton.

bear leader – a traveling tutor for young men going on a grand tour of Europe. He was called this since he led students on their trips as if they were trained bears.

beau monde – means the good or beautiful world and is another word for the ton (see ton below).

beaux – usually in the Regency, this referred to dandies (see dandy below).

bedizened – dressed or adorned in a showy, gaudy or tasteless manner.

Bedlam – the insane asylum in London where people would go to see the inmates as we might go today to look at animals in a zoo for entertainment. Its real name, when founded in the 1400s, was the Hospital of St. Mary of Bethlehem, but that name had long ago been corrupted, first into Bethlehem Hospital, and then into Bedlam which is why bedlam today means a scene or state of wild and noisy uproar or confusion.

benevolence – the desire to promote the happiness of others; goodwill; kindly feeling or an act of kindness; something good that is done **or** a generous gift.

besom – broom, usually one made of a bunch of twigs tied to a handle.

bespoke – engaged to be married; spoken for.

bishoping – altering a horse's teeth with a file to make the horse appear younger and thus deceive the prospective buyer.

bit o'muslin – a woman who exchanges sexual favors for money – a prostitute.

black book – to be in someone's black book was to be seriously out of favor.

blacklegs – touts or bookies at sporting events who take bets on those events.

blades – dashing, swaggering or jaunty young men.

bloat – dead body in the water, so-called because a body left in water swells up and then rises to the surface.

bloods – high-spirited dandies; adventurous youths; more negatively, profligates or rakes.

blood sports – hunting and even riding to hounds, staples of aristocratic country life.

blow a cloud – smoke (but never in the presence of women).

blue devils – the state of being truly depressed; depression; the mopes.

blue stocking – a woman interested in books, in learning and all educational pursuits. From the so-called "Blue Stocking Society" a group of society ladies who first met in the 1750s to discuss literature and other topics that society did not think it proper for women to discuss. Interestingly, the "blue stockings" were worn by a man, Benjamin Stillingfleet, who was asked by the ladies to attend the group. Since he didn't own formal evening dress nor the black stockings required with such dress, he wore his usual informal clothes to the group's meetings along with blue worsted stockings. The term is usually used in denigration of women interested in intellectual pursuits.

blue ruin – gin, the drug of the poor because it was cheap.

blunt – money; ready cash.

bonhomie – good nature; geniality.

bon ton – the topmost members of society (see ton below).

Boodle's – the third oldest men's club on St. James Street in London. It was founded in the Regency for younger, conservative men of the "landed gentry" who are not peers but are baronets, knights, or squires (see White's and Brooks's below).

bosom-bow – an intimate or confidential friend, a phrase used by women to describe such a person or by men in the plural to describe two women who were very close friends.

bottom – courage, pluck.

boulanger – a baker of bread and other non-sweetened baked goods.

brace (of pistols) – a matched pair, often of dueling pistols.

brangle – a squabble or to squabble; to dispute in an angry or noisy manner (usually Cant).

brazen – shameless or impudent.

breach of promise – If one's fiancé broke off the engagement, the injured party could sue for breach of promise and possibly receive a financial settlement from the courts in restitution for the social disgrace of being rejected.

Bristol Man – an insult implying the person is either low class or acting that way. It may be based on the person's accent not being acceptable to the person making the judgment or a behavior that is not acceptable. It came from Bristol's connection to the sea, sailors, and the shipping trade, all of which had a bad reputation.

British Museum – This had existed since 1753 and opened to the public in 1759. It was the first museum in England where the entire collection belonged to the nation. The information on the collections was available within its Reading Room. The first students' room, one containing Prints and Drawings, opened in 1808. The museum was housed in Montagu House in Bloomsbury during the Regency and didn't begin to move into its new building until the Victorian Age when the increase of its many collections led to its current building, the first phase opening in 1852. The books in the collection are now housed in a new building near St. Pancras Railway Station that opened in 1993.

Brooks's – the second oldest men's club in London to which those of the ton who were more liberal and favored the Whig party could be elected. There they could talk politics, find refuge, and gamble. It was and is on St. James Street, a street women did not frequent (see White's below and Boodle's above).

brougham – a four-wheeled, boxlike, closed carriage for 2-4 persons having a driver's perch outside as well as footmen's stands on the back and pulled by at least two horses.

brown (or doing it up brown) – deceived; taken in, the image being that of being roasted.

brown study – when someone is referred to as being in a brown study, this means the person is in a reverie, deep in thought, or in a dark mood.

buck – impetuous, dashing and spirited man or youth

bully back – a physically intimidating man hired by a brothel to intimidate and remove customers who were causing problems such as drunks and other troublemakers, what we would call a bouncer (see flashman below).

bruit – to voice abroad; to spread a report or rumor of.

brunnish – showy but inferior and worthless.

brush and lope – to run away - lower class slang.

budget – as in "open her budget" meaning mouth.

bumblebroth – a tangled situation; a mess.

butler – did more than answer doors. He was also responsible for directing the male servants of the household staff (except those under the male chef if there was one) and sometimes the female staff as well, along with the housekeeper. His duties also included overseeing the security of the household, protecting the silver, and supervising the service at meals to see that all was done according to the correct protocol. He also assisted in the hiring of new staff (see also cook, footman, tiger, housekeeper and maids).

buy old boots – marry another man's mistress.

by-blow – an illegitimate child.

C

cabriolet – a lightweight, two-wheeled carriage that seated two people and often had a folding top. It was drawn by just one horse which made it less expensive to maintain which was why it replaced the curricle (see curricle below) later in the period as the fashionable young man's favorite form of transportation.

cacophony – harsh, dissonant sound (ex: There was a cacophony of hooting, cackling and wailing heard from the crowd.) or a discordant and meaningless mixture of sound (ex: the cacophony of city traffic at rush hour).

cad – one who behaves in a dishonorable or irresponsible way toward women.

calomel – a white powder used in the 1800s as a purgative (laxative) and as a fungicide to treat yellow fever. It was tasteless but dangerous as it contained a form of mercury.

cambric – a fine, thin linen or cotton cloth used for women's clothes and sometimes for men's shirts.

canny –sly; shrewd and cautious in dealing with others; thrifty.

caper merchant – dancing instructor.

Captain Sharp – a person who cheats.

care-for-naught – a selfish person; a empty-headed person.

Carleton House fete – name used for any party that resembled the orgies reputed to be held by the Prince Regent and his intimates at that house in London.

Carleton House set – name given to the group of the Prince Regent's close friends who often met at Carleton House, the Prince's house on Pall Mall. Many were men of ill repute.

carte blanche – an offer by a "gentleman" that includes living under his protection but not marriage. (See Foreign Dictionary (mostly French) at www.carolgoss.com for more information.)

cast up one's accounts – to vomit.

caterwauling – howling or screeching like an angry or frightened cat.

cattle – in the Regency, this refers to horses, though "cattle" can also refer to other domesticated four-footed farm animals as well (see prads below).

cattle stud – a business considered proper for a gentlemen where he bred and raised horses.

cavalier behavior – carefree, nonchalant, or jaunty behavior, often used as a cover, especially when one's feelings have been hurt.

cavil – to object in a trivial and irritating manner; to find fault with something for no real reason; as a noun, it is such an objection.

caught on the raw – made upset and angry as in "What's caught you on the raw?"

cent-per-cent man – a moneylender, actually a loan shark, as the interest is 100% of principal, thus costing the borrower a cent of interest for every cent borrowed.

chaise longue – literally "a long chair", it is a chair with a long seat so one can lay back in it and relax with one's legs stretched out as if sitting on a bed. It should never be referred to as a "chaise lounge."

chaperone – a respectable woman in charge of an unmarried young lady particularly in a public setting.

charlatan – (see humbug below).

chatelaine – the mark of office of a housekeeper, it was often elaborate and held a collection of keys that would open every room in the house and which she wore at her waist. It meant she was trusted so highly as to be able to enter any space in the house on her own without specific instructions or an escort.

cheeseparing – stingy, often used for an object of no value save in the eyes of a miser.

Cheltenham tragedy – anything that is melodramatic and overdone. This is probably a Heyerism (see Heyerism below); however, there were a number of lesser theatres in Cheltenham at this time where both the plays and especially the acting were considered to be of a mediocre quality so the term is appropriate.

chemise – a loose, shirt-like garment worn under their dresses by Regency women and girls. Sometimes it had sleeves, sometimes it didn't, depending on the style of gown. It tied in the front with a drawstring or ribbons and was often of lightweight fabric. If a woman wore stays (a light, often short corset) it was worn over the chemise. However, most Regency ladies wore neither petticoats nor drawers, though drawers came more into acceptance as the period got closer to its end (see drawers, petticoats, and stays below).

cheroot or cigarillo – a small, thin cigar. Smoking was not very popular among men in the Regency. Most of the men who smoked picked up the habit in Spain while fighting during the Peninsular War.

chit – (as person) a child or young person especially a pert girl.

chit – (as thing) a signed note for money owed for food, drink, etc.; any voucher or receipt of an informal nature.

cicisbeo – 18th century word, still used at times in 1800s, for the escort or lover of a married woman. Remember, marriage based on love is still, for most people, a radical idea in the Regency (see marriage below).

cits – citizens (used negatively) for a resident of the City, the area of London where banks and businesses are located and often where such persons lived. Used by some members of the ton when referring to the middle or merchant class, even when these men were fabulously wealthy, as the ton often looked down on those men because they had earned their wealth rather than inheriting it and had no titles.

City – The City (always capitalized) was and still is the financial center of London. It runs along the north side of the Thames river from the Tower of London west to Temple Bar and dates from the Roman period when this was the settlement the Romans called Londinium.

clement – (opposite of inclement) – compassionate; In weather – mild; balmy; pleasant.

clerk – a person employed in an office to keep accounts or records, write out letters, and other duties as required (Think Bob Cratchit in Dicken's *A Christmas Carol*) **or** a layman who has minor church duties. The word clerk is pronounced "clark".

climbing boy – a young, slightly built, poor boy often sold into servitude to a chimney sweep who used the child to climb up into the narrow, hard-to-reach parts of a chimney regardless of the danger. They usually died at a young age from the dangers of their work and/or ill treatment by their owners during the latter part of the Regency and into the Victorian age (see mudlark or skylark below).

clodpole – a stupid person.

close as wax – miserly, stingy, secretive.

clutch-fisted – miserly.

cock up one's toes – to die.

coffee houses – where men went to drink coffee, read the newspapers of the day and enter into lively discussions about topics like politics, the arts or horseracing. They also served food. Some still existed in London even after the famous men's clubs like White's, Brooks's and Boodle's became fixtures in Regency life.

collect – (see recollect below).

colly-wobbles – slang term for a stomach ache.

come out – the first entry of a young lady into society, what we would call her debut. If of the ton and thus a daughter of the peerage (see peer below), she could first be presented at the Royal Court though not all did this. A ball would then be held in her honor, or she would come out at the ball held for this purpose at Almack's (see Almack's above). After that, she could attend society events and seek a suitable husband at those events.

come up to scratch – said of a man who made an offer of marriage, willingly or not.

confinement – in the latter stages of pregnancy, when they could not hide it with their clothes, women withdrew from society. They did not receive any but their closest female friends though they sometimes could attend a small dinner in their own home until near the end of the pregnancy. This was more strictly enforced by society in Victorian times than in the Regency.

conge – to give someone his or her conge is to dismiss that person from your life and any relationship with him or her. Especially done to men who have done something wrong toward a woman or for a man to use to get rid of a mistress or lover.

convivial – fond of eating and drinking with friends; jovial; sociable or suitable for a feast or a banquet; festive.

consols – short for Consolidated Annuities. These were government securities that paid a fixed rate of interest each year and so were considered a most secure investment.

cook – rules the kitchen and is equal to the butler and housekeeper in status. She or he has a number of servants as kitchen staff under his or her control.

Corinthian – a gentleman of the ton who led a dissolute and luxurious lifestyle of wealth, licentious behavior, and dressed in the highest of fashion, even to the point of starting new fashions himself. He was also devoted to horse racing, pugilism (see pugilism below) and other dangerous sports such as racing curricles (see curricles below) or phaetons (see phaetons below) on open roads at great danger to himself and others. The name comes from the belief that the people of Corinth in ancient Greece lived luxurious and licentious lives.

cork-brained – foolish, stupid. A person like this was referred to as a cork-brain.

corn – refers to all major cereal crops, so a field of any grain is a corn field. American corn is referred to as maize.

corpulent – large or bulky of body; fat.

costermonger – one who peddles fruits and vegetables from a cart on the street. Also called a coster, this term dates from 1820 or later (see barrow boy or girl above).

cotillion – a formal ball for a young lady as her come out ball (see come out above) **or** a social dance with a variety of elaborate and stately steps and figures performed by four or more couples. It was led by one couple and involved changing of partners often.

country dance – where partners face each other in two long lines and then weave patterns as they move. This type of dancing originated in the rural areas of England, hence its name.

coup de grace – in both French and English, it is an action which puts a finish to something or someone or an action that gives a person or an animal a merciful death.

cove – a man who is most likely a rogue and of the lower classes.

Covent Garden Theatre – one of only two theatres (see Theatre Royal, Drury Lane below) in London during the Regency allowed to present straight theatre which meant plays with dialogue but no music. The theatre on this site during the Regency was built in 1809 after the first one had burned down. Plays were performed here but also ballets and opera as well as the occasional specialty act.

coxcomb – a vain, conceited and foolish man.

crim con – In a case of adultery, the wronged husband could file a civil suit against the man who had "seduced" his wife and could be awarded financial damages. The legal term for the charges brought was "criminal conversation." For rakes and rogues of the Regency, "crim con" charges were a real danger to both their reputations and their pocketbooks.

Crockford's – this was a gambling club founded late in the Regency (1828) and was referred to as the queen of gambling clubs. It is recorded that as much as 20 thousand pounds was lost and won in a single evening. Some men even lost their entire fortunes to gambling in this period of history as gambling was a major "sport".

crux (as in "the crux of the matter") – the essential part; the most important part; a puzzling or perplexing question; a difficult point to explain.

cry pax – cry peace.

curate – a clergyman who is the deputy or assistant to a pastor, a rector or a vicar.

curricle – a two-wheeled vehicle drawn by two horses, it was fast, maneuverable and driven mostly by fashionable young men with superb horses. It held the same place in the Regency as the sports car does today. It was replaced later by the cabriolet (see cabriolet above).

cut – to cut is to refuse to recognize a person socially by acting as if they don't exist. This was a terrible insult to the person at whom the cut was directed. The cut direct was the most humiliating to the person you wished to cut; you look the person directly in the face but pretend not to see her or him. The cut indirect is simply looking the other way. The cut sublime is looking up at the sky until the person passes. The cut infernal is looking at the ground or bending down to adjust your shoes or hem until the person passes.

cutting a dash – being famous due to one's fashionable dress, one's exploits, or one's conquests.

cynosure – something that strongly attracts attention by its brilliance, interest, etc. It can be used in both the positive and the negative sense.

Cyprian – one of many names for a courtesan. Others are "high flyer", "bird of paradise", or member of the demimonde. It was used to refer to a courtesan or a mistress rather than a common prostitute or streetwalker.

D

damned hum – false rumor, lie, trick, etc.

dandy – a man who is fastidious about his clothing and appearance.

darken one's daylights or just one's lights – give a black eye.

darkling – used to describe a glance that is vaguely threatening or menacing; can also mean obscure.

debt of honor – at clubs, for gambling and wagers. Must be paid before any other debts or the gentleman would lose his standing in society.

debutante – a young lady (usually about 17) who had polished all her social graces and was ready for her come out – to be presented by her parents or guardians to society.

décolletage – a very low neckline on a woman's gown.

delimit – fix or mark the limits or boundaries of something.

delope – fire skyward in a duel as a refusal to kill, often an insult to the opponent. Might be done if the person thought the duel stupid or if he really did not want to harm the other man. However, he risked being killed by the other man for doing so.

demimonde – literally "the half word or underworld", it refers to the class of prostitutes who usually are courtesans or mistresses but can refer to the class of women who have been ruined and have had to move into that world. The word for a member of this class is demimondaine.

Derby – one of the three major horse races in England during the Regency. It took place at Epson Downs. In fact, it still does today. The race was and is pronounced Darby (see Newmarket and St. Leger below).

detritus – an accumulation of small fragments, such as sand or silt, worn away from rock; any disintegrated material, even of the mind or of one's actions.

deuced – a more polite way to call someone or something "damned"; it is pronounced " deu–ced in two syllables with the accent on the first syllable.

Devil's daughter – a termagant; a violent, scolding, quarreling woman as in, "He married the Devil's daughter."

devil to pay – really serious trouble as in "There will be the devil to pay when this comes out."

diamond of the first water – an extremely beautiful woman; a woman who is perfect according to the current fashion.

dicked in the nob – crazy (usually Cant).

disguised – drunk as in "He was a trifle disguised." This may also be a Heyerism (see Heyerism below).

dogcart – a country vehicle with two wheels, it held one or two people and was pulled by just one horse. It got its name from the ventilated box under the seat where the owner could put his hunting dogs on the way to the field or the fox hunt. The box was also useful for transporting other goods when not transporting dogs. In addition, it had a folding bench that would seat two more people if needed.

doing the pretty – said of a male, usually an eligible one, who is at a function being attentive and charming to the eligible young women present whether he wants to or not.

dolly mop – a prostitute. Originally, the word meant mistress but in this period means harlot.

domino – a long, hooded cloak worn over one's clothes and also with a mask over one's face when attending a masquerade, most especially a licentious one (see masque below).

dowager – refers to the widow of a peer. Generally it is only used if the current male holder of the title is married, and therefore, the female title (for example, the Countess of Essex) refers to the peer's wife. However, some mothers of peers used the title of Dowager Countess to pressure their unmarried heir into a marriage they wanted to take place.

dower house – a relatively smaller house on an estate to which the dowager would retire when the new heir took up residence or, if he was unmarried, at least when he married.

doxy-whore – an old-fashioned word to use in the Regency.

drab – when used as a noun for a woman means she is a slattern, a dirty and/or untidy woman.

draft – (see bankdraft above).

draper – a seller of fabrics.

draw someone's claret – give someone a bloody nose as claret was a red wine.

drawers – ladies' underpants with a drawstring waist, legs that came at or below the knee and an open crotch so that the person could take care of her personal needs without having to struggle with her skirt and chemise (see chemise above and stays below). For most of the Regency, ladies did not wear drawers nor did men. They were considered vulgar. As the Regency drew to its end, women began to wear them, and in the Victorian era, they were required to be worn and lengthened to the ankles.

drawing room – a shortening of the earlier phrase, withdrawing room, it is a formal room for receiving visitors and the place to which ladies would "withdraw" to have tea after dinner. As a rule, the men stayed at the dinner table drinking port for a while and then went to drawing room to join the ladies for the rest of the evening's social time.

droll – humorous but in a rather odd and whimsical way.

dudgeon – bad mood.

duel – usually fought in the Regency with pistols rather than swords and meant to settle disputes of "honor". A challenge would be issued by the person who was offended or who was defending someone else, such as his family or a lady. The person who had offended could then apologize, or the two opponents would have to meet on the "field of honor." Dueling was illegal in England but rarely prosecuted as most participants were members of the upper class while the prosecutors and police were not. The location and time of the duel was negotiated by the "seconds", friends or close acquaintances of the participants who, according to the rules of dueling, would have to fight in a participant's place if he did not show at the time and place set. This almost never happened as a man would be totally disgraced if he didn't show up. The rules of dueling also required the presence of at least one surgeon to give immediate medical care to the wounded (if he was not already dead). Famous Regency figures who participated in duels included Byron, Fox, Pitt, Canning and Wellington. Dueling is also referred to as an affair of honor.

drum – an assembly of the upper class, called the ton, at a private house in the evening.

dunderhead – (see shallowpate below).

dun territory – to be in dun territory is to be heavily in debt; lacking funds.

E

ebullient – overflowing with excitement, liveliness; very enthusiastic; boiling; bubbling.

economist – a stingy person.

effervescent – lively; bubbling; sparkling.

embruted – descended to the level of a brute.

enervated – weakened; lacking strength or vigor.

ensorcel - to bewitch someone (from en + sorcerer).

entail – to limit the inheritance of property attached to the title to the legitimate heir, usually the eldest son. Such property cannot be passed on to anyone else, though money can be. This law worked to keep great estates intact for centuries.

ept – socially, it is the opposite of inept.

equipage – one's carriage or the carriage with its horses, driver, and servants.

escritoire – writing desk, especially that of a lady.

expectations – a person's future financial or career prospects, often asked by a father or guardian of any man wishing to marry his daughter or ward.

F

fall – Regency trousers did not have a fly as we know it. Instead, there was a button at the waistband and a square opening over the crotch area. The fall was a piece of material that extended from the legs to cover the square opening and buttoned on either side at the waist. It could be dropped for whatever purpose the man had in mind.

false calves – pads inserted to fill out a man's stockings when he was wearing knee breeches but did not have the figure to look good in such clothing. These were never, of course, worn by a hero in a romance.

Fancy – the Fancy referred to enthusiasts of a sport, especially pugilism. Pugilism was often illegal, bare-knuckle boxing matches and even championships, regularly watched by crowds of between 3,000 -10,000. These were marathon bouts of great violence frequently fought in and around London. The competition was not over until one man was unconscious. That could take hours and even result in death.

farewell – to farewell a person or group was the phrase used to describe saying goodbye and seeing that person or group off.

faro – a card game where players bet on the order in which the cards will appear when dealt from the bottom of the deck. (See, I told you Regency men would bet on anything.)

fat-pocketed – a person whose wealth was either under-handedly or illegally gotten.

featherman – a person hired to march in a funeral procession to add to its impressiveness.

febrifuge – something to dispel or reduce a fever; such a medicine or agent or a cooling drink.

febrile – feverish; marked by fever.

feckless – ineffective; futile; spiritless; worthless.

fichu – a scarf-like item of lace or other lightweight, filmy fabric tucked into the neckline of a lady's dress to make the neckline more modest.

fives – a fist; "Handy with his fives" means a man is a good boxer.

flash cove – (Cant) a dangerous swindler who leads another into bad company.

flash her or his hash – (Cant) vomit.

flashman – see "bully back" above.

Fleet prison – this was the debtor's prison of London where people who couldn't pay their debts were incarcerated until those debts were paid. Peers, however, were not put in prison for debt (see peer below).

foolscrap – writing paper of the Regency.

footman – male servant under a butler. Served at dinner, attended ladies of the house on errands and social calls, and looked after candles and lamps in the house. They wore old-fashioned livery in the style of the 18th century, usually including a powdered wig. They were usually 6 feet tall or taller in order to impress their employer's friends and

A REGENCY LEXICON FOR READERS AND WRITERS

acquaintances. However, because the country was at war during the Regency and needed all able-bodied men it could get to fight Napoleon, there was a high tax placed on male servants. Thus, having footmen during Regency conferred high status on the family that had them. Also, during the war, there might be younger boys who did some of this work, men with disabilities of a minor nature and older men who came back to work for a family to fill in.

footpad – mugger; street robber.

fop – a gentleman who dresses in extremely elaborate clothes and puts on affected manners. The word is an insult.

forfend – (1) to defend, secure or protest; (2) to fend off, avert or prevent (3) to forbid.

fortnight – two weeks is a fortnight (see sennight below).

foxed – well and truly drunk.

frank – a Member of Parliament, including peers in the House of Lords, could mail letters free of charge by placing his personal seal along with writing the word "frank" or "free" on the outside of the letter. As envelopes were rarely used and most letters were just folded and addressed on the outside of the paper, that was where the address was placed if the letter was mailed rather than hand-delivered by a footman as it might be in London or other large town. The practice of franking continued until 1840, when cheap postal rates were introduced. This franking privilege is still used, however, in the U.S.A. by senators and congress members of both the federal and state governments.

fraud – (see humbug below).

fraught – loaded or filled with, as in "fraught with danger."

freebooter – one who robs and plunders, especially pirates and smugglers.

French leave – to go off without taking leave of the company, used in the Regency to refer to people who have run away to the countryside or even left the British Isles entirely to escape from their creditors.

French letter – a condom usually made of a thin leather like goat skin and which tied on to a man's penis with ribbons.

fribble – a silly, useless person or an effeminate fop.

Friday-faced – having a glum or dismal facial expression. This seems to be a Heyerism (see Heyerism below).

funds – usually referred to as being " in the funds." These were government securities that could be purchased by investors and were considered safe investments.

fustian – bombastic language; made up of pompous, high-sounding language, as in "It's fustian nonsense." It can also mean a coarse, heavy cloth of cotton and flax.

G

gainsay – deny, contradict, dispute (gainsaid – past tense).

gambling hell – a club for gambling and drinking where one did not have to be elected a member. Here a young or innocent person, referred to by the experienced as a "pigeon", was more likely to fall victim to a dishonorable "shark" than at an elite gentlemen's club like White's or Brooks's or Boodle's though one could lose one's fortune in either type of club (see Crockford's above).

gaming cant – terms used by gamblers in the Regency such as:

* children in the wood – dice.

* cleaned out – having lost all your money, beaten, ruined.

A REGENCY LEXICON FOR READERS AND WRITERS

* dispatchers – false dice.

* elbow shaker – a gamester casting dice.

* Fulhams – loaded dice.

* gulled – deceived or cheated.

* gullgropers – money lenders; cent per centers (see cent per cent man above).

* hatches – in debt (usually stated as being 'under the hatches').

* hell – (see gambling hell above).

* high-flyers – gamblers for high stakes.

* legs – bookmaker (see blacklegs above).

* nick – to win at dice or hit the mark just in the nick of time.

* (the) ready – the money.

* vowel – a written acknowledgement of a debt of honor (see vowels below).

gammon – as a noun: nonsense; humbug; as a verb: to deceive, to tell lies.

garret – attic, usually a small, wretched one.

gauze – a thin, filmy fabric. When used for women's gowns, it was in layers so the gown would not be so transparent.

gazetted (rake or womanizer) – usually a rake well-known to many from his exploits being reported in the newspapers of the time called gazettes.

Gentleman Jackson – was a famous pugilist (bare-knuckles boxer) and won the title Champion of England in 1795. He then opened a boxing academy next door to Angelo's Fencing Academy on Bond Street at #13. It was the favorite of

Regency aristocrats. In fact, it was considered an honor to spar with Jackson himself. Jackson was noted for his gentlemanly manners and dress (see Angelo's Fencing Academy above).

gentry – usually referred to as "landed" gentry. These were wealthy men but not peers. Instead they were men such as baronets, knights or squires.

gig – a light, open, two-wheeled carriage pulled by one horse which could seat two people and was often used in the country.

gin punch – a low class drink that can also be used as an astringent.

give his horses the office – signal a team of horses to move forward.

governess – basically a babysitter or trainer for a young girl. She kept the girl out of trouble, educated her in "accomplishments" and taught her how to behave like a true lady so she could land a suitable husband of her class or hopefully of a higher class than her own (see accomplishments above).

green girl – an inexperienced young lady.

grouse – a game bird that lives on the moors and is a favorite target of enthusiastic hunters along with their dogs. Blood sports were a basic activity of aristocratic country life.

guinea – the standard gold coin until 1813 when it was replaced by the sovereign. It equaled one pound plus one shilling or 21 shillings as there were 20 shillings to the pound (see sovereign below).

guise – style of dress or garb or outward appearance; aspect; semblance or assumed appearance; pretense.

greatcoat – a man's long, outdoor overcoat which usually had several capes over the shoulders to protect the wearer from rain or snow.

Gretna Green – a town just over the border in Scotland where eloping couples went to marry because you needed no license, no waiting period, and no consent from parent or guardian. You didn't even need a minister; anyone could be a witness. One of the usual places to marry was the blacksmith's forge. Thus the famous phrase developed for such a marriage of being "married over the anvil."

gudgeon – one who is easily imposed on or taken in (named after a small, carp-like fish that is easily caught).

gull – as noun: person who is easily cheated or taken in.

gull – as verb: deceive; cheat; impose on.

H

haberdashery – sells trim, threads, buttons and other items for clothing.

hackney – a coach or carriage for hire, especially in a city where it was used as a taxi cab.

ha-ha – a drop off or dip in the landscape. It can't be seen until you're almost on top of it. Because of this, it doesn't spoil the view but works even better than a fence to keep cattle, sheep or other animals away from the house and the landscaping near it.

half-pay officer – British army or naval officer paid a reduced amount since he is not on active duty at that time or is retired from service.

ham-fisted or cow-handed – clumsy.

harridan – a bad-tempered, disreputable old woman.

havey-cavey – a very late Regency or Victorian street word for "up to no good".

hazard – a dice game that was an earlier and more complicated version of the more modern game of craps. Although illegal, it was a chief gambling game, and playing it ruined the fortunes of numerous Regency gentlemen. It was especially popular at Crockford's (see Crockford's above).

heavy wet – ale.

hell – (see gambling hell above).

hell-bent – describes a person impetuously or recklessly determined to do something or to achieve something.

henwit – nitwit (especially a woman); a silly young woman.

Hessians – popular, polished leather boots for gentlemen in the Regency, they came up to just below the knee and often had tassels at the top. They fit snugly and thus were often difficult to remove without help.

Heyerism – a word thought to have been invented by Georgette Heyer, one of the most famous writers of romance novels in the earlier 20th century, many of whose novels are still in print. Ms. Heyer mixed real Regency words with those she invented. Thus many of her invented words are used by other writers today and accepted as a convention of the romance genre.

high in the instep – conceited; vain; snobbish.

high-kick gentleman – one who is dressed in the most up-to-date fashion; the top of fashion.

high stickler – one who is very proper or stiffly snobbish.

Hoare's Bank – an important bank during the Regency. It had been operating at 37 Fleet Street since 1690.

Hoby – a famous maker of men's boots, especially the Hessian style (see Hessians above).

hoity – giddy; flighty or inclined to put on airs; haughty.

hors de combat – in French, it is literally "out of the fight". In English it means the same but can also mean disabled or knocked down.

hors de loi – In French and English, it means outside the law and is often applied in England to a duel as they were illegal in the Regency (see duel above).

houri – one of the young, eternally beautiful women of the Muslim paradise, used in the Regency to describe a woman one finds tempting and irresistible.

housekeeper – the highest ranking female servant, she was responsible for everything in a great house including all the cleaning, the laundry, and all household maintenance. She thus supervised the huge number of maids it took to keep a great house running smoothly. The only thing she did not control was the kitchen and the cook. The triumvirate of butler, housekeeper and cook were the top dogs of the servant hierarchy and equal to each other. Around the housekeeper's neck or at her waist, she wore a "chatelaine" containing the keys to the entire household (see chatelaine above).

hoyden – a girl who is carefree, boisterous or tomboyish in her behavior. This is not used as a compliment.

hugger-mugger – (n) disorder; a confused situation; secrecy; (adj) clandestine; secretive (v) to act stealthily or secretively.

hullabub – disturbance; uproar.

hum – nonsense; not true or real; false or a sham.

humbug – a person who tries to deceive or cheat. Also called a fraud, a mountebank or a charlatan.

hussy – a term used most often by women usually for a bad-mannered or pert girl or, more severely, for an indecent or immoral woman.

I

I'll stand your friend – I'll be your friend; I'll stay your friend regardless of the situation.

imbroglio – a complicated or difficult situation; a mess of a situation or a complicated misunderstanding or disagreement.

impeccable – perfect; free from fault; irreproachable.

I'm rather more than seven – meaning, "Don't treat me like a child" or "Don't try to bam me."

in a trice – very quickly.

incessant – never stopping; continual; repeated without interruption.

inchoate – lacking order; just begun.

incipient – rudimentary; not yet completed or fully developed.

incomparable – often used to refer to a perfectly beautiful young lady of eligible age.

inexpressibles – men's breeches or trousers which usually fit tightly to the figure and showed off the man's assets. The name comes from the fact that it was not polite to mention them by their real name (see pantaloons below).

ingénue – a naive, artless young woman.

ingenuous – frank and open; free from restraint or reserve; sincere; simple and natural; innocent; naive. This is not necessarily a compliment.

in one's cups – drunk.

insouciant (noun -insouciance) – having the quality of being free from concern, worry, or anxiety; carefree, nonchalant; lighthearted, debonair, jaunty, breezy.

in the boughs – high or drunk.

It's an apparent bouncer – It seems to be an unlikely story or a lie.

It's all the kick – it is the high fashion of the moment; it is all the rage among the upper classes.

ivory turner – a person who is a cheater.

J

jackanapes – an insolent, rude and mischievous person.

jack-pudding – a male weakling.

jade – a disreputable and shrewish woman; a worthless woman.

jalap – a purgative, it was a light yellowish powder from morning glories and was used to treat yellow fever in early 1800s French Louisiana.

jarvey – a hackney coachman (see hackney above).

jaw-me-dead – a person who talks too much or sometimes, one who says things he shouldn't.

Jericho – to wish someone "to Jericho" is to wish them far away from you. It can also mean a place of concealment such as where someone hides that which he does not want others to know about, such as the location of an orgy or where he keeps a mistress he is not proud of. Thus something the person does not want anyone to know about.

jilt – a jilt was the derogatory term applied to a female who calls off an engagement. Doing so could seriously damage her reputation.

jointure – a legal financial arrangement for a widow. Typically the amount to be left to her if her husband dies is negotiated before her wedding based on the wealth she brought to the marriage and is thus established as a legal part of the marriage settlement.

jug bitten – suffering from a hangover. This seems to be one of the few words for this condition in the Regency which is odd considering the amount the men often drank in a day as the water, especially in the cities, was not safe to drink.

L

ladybird – often of the demimonde. A man's kept mistress or lover.

landau – the carriage most used by ladies for a ride in the park as it had two hoods which could cover all four passengers if the weather turned bad, or be left open to enable the passengers to view the sights, talk to their friends in other carriages or show off their new gowns or other finery. It was a luxury vehicle and so declared your wealth to all who saw you in it. Thus it was the favorite vehicle of ladies of the ton (see ton below) to ride in during their afternoon rides in Hyde Park in London.

lantern loo table – a table specifically designed to play the card game of loo, a popular game during the Regency (see loo below).

laudanum – liquid opium, the only effective drug for pain but highly addictive and dangerous.

leading strings – cloth strips fastened to the clothes of tiny children so adults could hold on to them and help a child learn to walk. Thus the phrase, "I'm not still in leading strings" meant "Don't treat me like a toddler." or "I'm not as naive as a young child."

le dernier cri – the newest fashion; the latest word; the latest thing.

leg-shackled – married. Males used this term, especially if not married themselves and trying to avoid it.

lexicon – a wordbook or dictionary, especially of Greek or Latin or the vocabulary of a particular language, field of study, social class, or person or an inventory or record of some area. This document is, therefore, a lexicon.

lightskirt – a prostitute, also called bachelor fare or Haymarket ware. These were more derogatory terms than demimonde, Cyprian or even ladybird.

limned – (1) represented in drawing or painting (2) portrayed in words; described.

Little Season – this was the autumn social season, coinciding with Parliament returning to work after the summer which it did not always do. Thus there was not always a Little Season during the year.

Long Meg – insulting term for a very tall woman but an ancient word in the Regency.

loo – a popular card game of the period in which a player who fails to take a trick must pay a fine or a forfeit (see lantern loo table above).

looby – an awkward person, especially one who is lazy or stupid; a lout; a lubber.

look lively – get a move on; in modern slang, "get the lead out!"

loose fish – an unreliable person who rarely distinguishes between truth and falsehood.

louring – lowering, as a cloud before a storm can be called a louring cloud.

Lud! – an exclamation = Lord! It was considered a more polite word to use.

lutestring (or lustring) – a type of silk used for making ladies' gowns, especially dressy ones, as this fabric flowed over the body but had enough firmness to make good collars and sleeves that held their shape.

M

Macaroni – English dandy (c. 1700s) who affected continental mannerisms, clothes, etc. The word was used during the Regency to refer to someone who was outlandishly dressed, especially in an out-of-date manner.

macau (or macao) – a card game like Crazy Eights but played with a standard 52 card deck where players play a single card in sequence. The game involved bluffing your opponent as well and unfortunately was a boon to players who chose to cheat.

madeira – a sweet white dessert wine often laced with brandy.

magistrate – a justice of the peace. Also, a police magistrate, the "judge" or official a suspected criminal was brought in front of after being arrested and who decided if the evidence was good enough for the person to be held for trial.

maids – female servants that rank as follows:

> * lady's maid – preferably French for status, got her lady's hand-me-downs as a perk.
>
> * housemaid – did the cleaning such as emptying chamber pots, cleaning fireplaces, and other household cleaning chores. These were usually the largest number of servants in a house.
>
> * kitchen maid – helped the cook to prepare food.
>
> * scullery maid – did all the dishes, pots and pans and kept

the kitchen clean and had the hardest job in the household.

* daily – a maid who lived out, not in-house as others did. Was lowest in rank as she most often worked for those who could not afford to have a live-in servant. She would be a temporary hire in a large house when extra help was needed if the master did not have enough staff in his employ elsewhere that he could bring in as needed for special events.

mail coach – a speedy coach which carried the mail on a regular schedule and on set routes. Part of what made it so fast was that it did not have to stop to pay tolls as other vehicles did on the toll roads. It occasionally carried a few passengers.

make an elegant leg – bow deeply and maybe a bit theatrically.

make an offer – to propose marriage to a woman.

make ducks and drakes – to squander money or potential money.

making a cake of oneself – making a fool of one's self, often over a member of the opposite sex.

malaise – a condition of general bodily weakness or discomfort that often marks the onset of a disease or a vague, unfocused feeling of mental uneasiness, discomfort, or lethargy.

Man of Mode – an obsessively fashion-conscious man. The label comes from a Restoration comedy of that name by George Etheredge and is a reference to the main character in the play called, in true Restoration style, Sir Fopling Flutter.

man-milliner – a homosexual man (see milliner below for the connection).

mantua maker – an older name for a dressmaker, it was used more in the early Regency (see modiste below).

marriage – the idea of marrying for love was a dangerous, revolutionary, and new idea at the time of the Regency. If the couple could treat each other with reasonable courtesy, the husband provided for his family, and the wife bore him children, especially an heir and a spare as it was referred to, that was pretty much what anyone expected of their marriage. In the old-style marriage, romance and passion were generally sought outside of marriage in the form of affairs with other married people or, for the man, by taking a mistress.

The idea of marrying for love was part of the 19th century's Romantic revolution which placed a higher value on emotions, an idea which had been scorned in the Age of Reason of the 18th century. The Romantics also placed a higher value on the individual whereas, previously, the individual was expected to acquiesce to his/her duty, stoically fulfilling the role in life assigned to him/her based on social rank/birth.

Of course, both ideologies coexisted in people's minds, especially in those of the young adults of the time. They were the ones in the thick of the fray of this cultural change. This gave many people an inner conflict over their values as they became torn between following traditional ways that had worked for hundreds of years versus the new idea of following their hearts. This inner conflict was reflected in many areas of life such as politics, music and art, architecture, literature and landscaping to name just a few (see also ciscebo above).

Marriage Mart – a term, mostly used by men who feared it, for the London Season when society mothers would launch their young daughters out into society to seek suitable husbands (see Season below).

masque (masquerade) – a costume ball. Some of these during the Regency were decadent affairs, even orgies, which is where the costumes worn came in handy and where a domino (see domino above) needed to be worn over one's costume when both entering and leaving in order to protect one's reputation, a precaution which, unfortunately, did not always work.

mawkish – sentimental.

megrims – migraine headache.

melancholia – depression, usually meaning the severe kind we refer to as clinical depression.

memoir – a personal narrative of facts and events experienced by the writer.

mercurial – sprightly and animated; quick or changeable; fickle.

mesmerized – the Regency term for being hypnotized, named for Franz Mesmer (1734-1815), Austrian physician who made it popular.

messuage – a medieval term for a house with its adjacent buildings and the lands attached to it for the use of the household (1350-1400) sometimes used by old families during the Regency to refer to their main estate and its lands.

mews – in medieval times and later, this was a building in which to keep hawks and falcons. In the Regency, many people in towns or cities lived in townhouses but needed a place to keep horses and carriages while in town. The mews was the carriage house which was at the back of the garden and faced the private alley behind the townhouse. Mews were smaller than stables.

Michaelmas – September 29, the feast of St. Michael the

Archangel. The autumn term at schools and universities is still, in England, referred to as the Michaelmas term. The names of the other terms vary between Oxford and Cambridge. As Oxford is the oldest, its terms start with Michaelmas, followed by Hilary term and Trinity term.

milk-and-water miss – an insipid girl devoid of interesting conversation.

mill – brawl or fight; in more formal terms, .a boxing match (see Fancy above and pugilism below).

milliner – a maker, usually a woman, of woman's hats, bonnets, and other head coverings.

mingle-mangle – a mess.

misalliance – a relationship or marriage with someone considered to be of lower social standing or otherwise unsuitable.

missish – prim; affected; prudish; squeamish; (also the noun missishness).

mistress – a formal word for a kept woman, said to be "under the protection" of her male keeper. If a girl was poor but beautiful, this was one route to a luxurious and fashionable, but insecure and disreputable life. As for men, there was no real social sanction against having a mistress if they could afford it. Wives might not love these arrangements, but in their culture, they were generally expected to turn a blind eye to them. There was the idea, which became even more strongly felt in the following Victorian period, that the wife, the mother of the children, was to be put on a pedestal. She was too "pure" to be an object of lust. She was to be what the Victorians referred to as the "angel of the home." The sultry, sexual role was saved for the mistress who, in turn, was not seen as being moral enough to be a good mother. Love and lust were often kept in separate compartments, as were the women who provided each. Respectable ladies and ladybirds generally were forbidden to speak to each other, even if they should, by chance, meet (aee marriage above).

modiste – the more fashionable name for a dressmaker during the Regency. Some even used French names to seem more fashionable (see mantua maker above).

monkey – 500 pounds in English money of the time.

mooncalf – a twit; a jerk; an idiot, referring to the old superstition that sleeping in the moonlight made a person insane which is why we have the word lunatic, literally one affected by luna, meaning moon.

mooted – If something was mooted, it was open to discussion or debate.

more hair than wit – said of a woman who is not very intelligent or clever.

mountebank – (see humbug above).

mudlark – (see climbing boy above).

muff chaser – a low class or Cockney term for a lecher.

mushroom – a derogatory word for a person who has suddenly come into wealth; an upstart; an allusion to the way mushrooms can spring up overnight on your lawn and seemingly out of nowhere (see toadstool below).

musicale – a music program forming the main part of a social occasion.

muslin – the most used fabric for Regency gowns, it could be white or colored, plain or embroidered, painted or otherwise decorated. Its greatest asset was that it was washable if not too decorated which, due to the harsh soaps available at time most other dress fabrics were not.

muslin company – prostitutes.

mute as a fish – silent.

N

nabob – a very rich man, especially one who acquired his fortune in India. One who tried and failed to do so or made very little money in this effort was referred to as a "chicken nabob."

nankeen – a strong, buff or yellow cloth made of cotton and named for Nanking, China from where it was first imported.

natal day – birthday.

Newgate Prison – the main prison in London and where prisoners were publicly executed, a common public spectacle in the Regency. It was attached to the Old Bailey (see Old Bailey below).

Newmarket – one of the three great horse races of the Regency was run here over four miles of roads and turf. Many gentlemen trained their horses here also (see Derby above and St. Leger below).

niffy-naffy – inclined to put on airs; haughty.

night chemise – garment worn to bed by a woman (from the French chemise du nuit). Also sometimes referred to as night clothes. The word "nightgown" was not in common usage at this time.

night rail – garment worn to bed by a woman. Some books use this word. Others do not.

ninnyhammer – fool or simpleton.

noblesse oblige – the obligation of persons of noble or high rank to behave nobly, honorably, and generously. This obligation was thought to be partly learned, partly inherited, and partly instinctive. If someone behaved this way who was not of this rank of society, she or he would often be referred to as a "natural lady or gentleman."

nodcock – fool.

nonesuch – one who is unequalled.

nous – (short for nous-box which means "head") – common sense, reason, mind, head, brain, or intellect.

nuncheon – another word for lunch.

nunnery – often called a Covent Garden nunnery, it meant a brothel.

nurse – person who cared for small children before they were put into the care of a governess or a tutor. It could also refer to a wet nurse whose job was to suckle the baby of a lady so the woman wouldn't have to lower her standards to do it herself. There were no official female nurses, even on the battle field, as we know them, until much later during Crimean War against the Russians when Florence Nightingale formed a true nurses' corps to take care of the British wounded.

nursery – usually located on the top floor of a residence, with all needed to care for children. It had rooms for the nurse, nanny, governess and any nursery maids, bedrooms for the children, play and schoolroom areas. Small children were usually not a regular part of their parents' lives but saw their parents, if at all, only at specific times of the day.

nursery maid – female servant whose job it was to help watch and clean up after the children.

O

of the first stare – in the most fashionable style.

Old Bailey – was located in the City (see City above) and in the Regency was the court where criminal cases for London and the county of Middlesex were tried though it now takes cases from across the country. It is an ancient court, though the building that housed it had been rebuilt many times by the Regency. Its name comes from the fact that its original building followed the City's old, fortified wall which was called a bailey. Newgate Prison is attached to it (see Newgate Prison above).

Old Lady of Threadneedle Street – the nickname of the Bank of England which is located on that street in the City (see City above). The bank has been there since 1734 and, during the Regency, the London Stock Exchange was there also. The name most likely comes from the medieval guild of the Merchant Taylors' Company. Their sign of three needles, which identified their Guild Hall, hangs to this day at # 30 Threadneedle Street.

on-dit – the word the ton used for gossip and rumor was referred to as this (see ton below).

on the River Tick – totally broke (see River Tick below).

on the shelf – beyond marriageable age; no longer wanted; used only about females.

opprobrium – disgrace or reproach brought on a person by shameful conduct; infamy; scorn; abuse or the cause or object of such reproach.

orgeat – a drink at social events. It was made of barley or almonds plus orange flower water and sugar. It was for those, mostly ladies, who did not favor alcoholic drinks or did not wish to be seen drinking alcoholic beverages in public for fear they might appear wanton and what was called "fast."

Original – an Original was a lady with a unique style – said half in admiration, half in derision.

out-and-outer – a person who does things with excessive thoroughness; an extremist or a thoroughgoing or perfect example of a kind or one who is excellent at something which needs a special skill.

outlier – person or thing that lies outside; person residing outside the place of business, duty, etc. As outliers, the word was used for outriders accompanying a carriage during a trip.

outré – in both French and English, it means exaggerated; overdone; extravagant; overstated.

P

Pall Mall – a game in which a ball is driven through a ring on a swivel, usually on a lawn. It may be an early version of croquet.

pannier – a basket, especially a large one for carrying goods, provisions, etc.; a basket for carrying items on one's back or panniers was a pair of them slung across the back of a beast of burden.

pantaloons – a later form of inexpressibles (see inexpressibles above). They usually fastened under the foot, inside or outside the boot, and fit tightly to the man's figure.

paper skull – not intelligent (probably Cockney rhyming slang for "dull").

paragon – an exemplary person; a model of correct behavior and integrity.

parson's mousetrap – another term unmarried men, and even

married ones, used for marriage.

parterre – in England, this was an ornamental arrangement of flower beds of differing sizes and shapes forming a garden.

patroness – mostly used in the Regency to refer to the specific women who ruled society and decided who did and who did not get vouchers for Almack's (see Almack's above).

parti – a person considered to be suitable as a marriage partner.

parure – a matched set of necklace, earring, bracelets and sometimes a brooch.

pattens – these were metal or wooden rings fastened with straps to the soles of shoes or boots to raise you above mud or slush or puddles, mostly worn by women.

pay your shot – pay your debts, especially your gambling debts which are debts of honor.

pedestrian curricle – a hobbyhorse on wheels, it is a type of cycle which a person propels with their feet on the ground as it has no pedals.

peer – a nobleman with a hereditary seat in the House of Lords: duke, marquess, earl, viscount, or baron are the only peers of the realm.

peignoir – in England, this usually refers to a woman's loose dressing gown, often one which is elaborate and sexy in its style.

pelisse – a woman's long outdoor cloak with either slits for arms or long sleeves. It was made like a dress but fastened in the front. It could be as long as the outfit underneath or a three-quarter length **or** the word sometimes was used for a robe a woman would wear over her nightclothes.

pelter – one who attacks with repeated blows or missiles or one who assails vigorously with words, questions, and such **or** one who hurries (in other words, pelts down the road, stairs, etc.).

perspicacious – keen in observing and understanding; discerning; shrewd.

petticoat – a skirt-like undergarment worn under a dress or gown like what we would call a half slip. In the early Regency, this garment was not often worn as the gown was to hang close to the body in a style modeled on the women's clothes of ancient Greece, Later on, they became regular wear as gowns became more elaborate and less molded to the figure.

phaeton – a light, four-wheeled carriage with front wheels smaller than those in the rear. It had no side protection either. The most popular were called high perch or high flyer phaetons. They had a very high seat which required a ladder to get into. This mode of transportation was rakish, fast, and brought the owner admiring attention from others, but it was terribly unstable and apt to tip over and thus dangerous to drive which, of course, only added to its appeal to young men.

physician vs. surgeon – a physician had gentleman status because he did not do manual labor as he did not touch the patient. He treated the person by questioning them on their symptoms and then writing out prescriptions to be made up by the local apothecary. The surgeon did everything from pulling teeth to amputation. Since he worked with his hands which were often covered with blood, particles of flesh and even dirt, he was considered a workman and thus of lower rank than a doctor. This former difference in rank is still visible today in Great Britain as physicians are given the title Dr. while surgeons are still referred to as Mr. though both are now respectable.

pianoforte – the real name of a piano and used in the Regency when it replaced, in many well-to-do households, the harpsichord which, although it was excellent for showing off precision, technical brilliance, and virtuosity of the player, was limited in emotional expressiveness as the player could not control the volume of the music as one could on the pianoforte. It also tended to stay in tune more often than the harpsichord.

pin money – a woman's yearly allowance given for personal purchases. The average sum given to a lady of the upper class or peerage was about 400-500 pounds sterling a year That is about $20,000 - $25,000 U.S. today – a huge sum considering that a governess made about 15 pounds a year. This sum could be written into her marriage settlement or just informally agreed to by her husband. The former was more secure as it was negotiated by her male relatives before the wedding as part of the wedding contract and thus was legally binding on the woman's husband.

piquant – agreeably pungent or sharp in taste or flavor; pleasantly biting or tart or agreeably stimulating, interesting or attractive as in a piquant glace or having a lively or interestingly provocative character as in having a piquant wit.

piquet – a card game played by 2 persons with a pack of 32 cards with deuces through sixes excluded.

plant a facer – punch someone in the face.

pluck – courage; spirit.

plump in the pocket – rich, wealthy.

poaching –illegally hunting game on a landowner's property, a crime punishable by transportation to a penal colony like

Australia. Landowners were permitted to ward off poachers by severe means such as setting man-traps or even shooting them.

pockets to let – broke; having no money.

po-faced – humorless and disapproving.

point non plus – broke; totally out of money with no options for acquiring more.

poltroon – a wretched coward.

pomander ball – old-fashioned ball of mixed aromatic substances to scent a cupboard or armoire. A common example today is an orange studded all over with cloves.

ponce – English word for a pimp.

pony – 25 pounds in English money of the time. This is a large sum as a governess would be well-paid at 15 pounds a year, as in Charlotte Bronte's novel, *Jane Eyre*.

poppet – a term of endearment, especially for a child.

popinjay – a twit, a fop.

port – the posture of a person **or** a sweet, heavy, red wine drunk almost exclusively by men, often after dinner when the ladies would leave for the drawing room to drink tea.

portmanteau – a suitcase or traveling bag.

posset – milk drink for children or those who were sick, served warm.

post-chaise – a small, closed, four-wheeled carriage that one could rent for long trips. Usually it had four seats inside.

post the cole – Cockney rhyming term for paying money you owe.

prads – (see cattle above).

precessed (in a waltz) – turning in the waltz thus spinning the lady in one's arms around one's body. This action was one of the reasons the waltz was seen originally as so scandalous for the dancers' bodies often touched in this maneuver.

pretentious – said of a person who makes an ass of himself/herself by making claims to excellence or importance that he/she does not have; doing things for show or to make a fine appearance; showy; ostentatious.

primogeniture – inheritance by the first born son. This consisted of putting the male firstborn in charge, educating him for that position, and assuming he would look out for his younger siblings responsibly since it was clear that any other pattern would lessen the amount of land the heir inherited and thus lessen the wealth of the family as land was considered the only real wealth. Younger sons of wealthy families were, in the 1800s, expected to make their own way in the world unless directly left money or unentailed land by the father. One solution to extra and younger sons was to send them into the military or the church.

Prinny – refers to the Prince of Wales, the Prince Regent and is often used in a somewhat disparaging way (see Carleton House fete and Carleton House set above).

proprieties – conventional standards of proper behavior and manners.

pudding shammer – (Cant) one who steals food to survive, considered among street people as the lowest of the low except for beggars who rank at the very bottom.

puffing – inflating with pride and vanity or to praise unduly or with exaggeration.

pugilism – illegal, bare hand boxing (see Fancy above).

punting on the River Tick or up the River Tick – broke; without funds and living on credit (see River Tick below).

putative – commonly regarded as; reputed to be; supposed to, as in, "He is a putative traitor."

Q

quadrille – a square-type dance of 4 couples consisting of 5 parts or movements, each complete in itself. In this dance, there are glissades (slides) and chasses (gliding steps).

quality – another term for the ton; the beau monde - the upper classes of society, the fashionable set (see ton below and beau monde above).

quarter day – the day at the end of each quarter of the year when rents were due and a person's allowance was paid to him either from his family or from a trust fund.

queer in the attic – peculiar; crazy; not quite all there.

Queer Street – to be in Queer Street was to be of doubtful solvency. In fact, you were probably marked in a tradesman's ledger with a "quaere" (inquire) which meant, "Make inquiries about this customer as he's not paying his bills."

quizzing glass – a magnifying glass worn on a chain or cord, often decorative as well as useful and used in place of spectacles (see spectacles below). Looking at someone through it could be used as a form of put-down if that is what the person wielding it desired.

R

Radcliffe novels – Gothic style novels / originally referring to the novels of Ann Radcliffe: *The Romance of the Forest* (1791)/ *The Mysteries of Udolpho* (1794)/ *The Italian* (1797). Later used to refer to any novels that contained romanticized views of nature, intimations of evil, and prolonged scenes of suspense.

rag-mannered – ill-mannered, presumably because one behaves with the poor manners of the lower classes such as beggars dressed in rags.

rake – a man who has all the vices such as drinking and gambling, who has attracted and, with his sexual conquests, "ruined" many women, though a gentleman rake will not ruin a lady who is a virgin, except by mistake. In that case, he will offer marriage to repair the damage he has caused to her reputation. Also called a "rakehell."

rapacious – plundering; grasping; greedy; living by the capture of prey; seizing by force; predatory.

rapscallion – rascal, rogue or scamp.

rattlepate – a giddy, empty-headed, talkative person.

rattletrap – person whose tongue runs on and on like it was on wheels.

Recamier couch – a couch with an arm only at one end to lean against.

receipt – a recipe for something. The word is still used this way in England.

Regency – Technically, the period from 1811-1820 in England when George III was not mentally competent to rule England and the business of the monarchy was carried out by the Prince of Wales (see Prinny above). However, it is often dated from about 1790-95 until 1837 as ideas, fashions and culture of this period left the Age of Reason and moved through the Romantic Age up to the ascension to the throne of Queen Victoria. Thus, novels labeled as Regency can be set at any time in this span.

resolve – to make up one's mind to; decide; be firm in one's purpose or clear away; dispel.

reticent – inclined to remain silent or to say little; reserved in speech.

reticule – a lady's soft handbag or purse with a drawstring top, usually made to match her outfit or dress and meant to hold the small essentials she would need at a dance or other occasion.

recollect – call back to mind; remember. The difference between recall and recollect is to recall something needs effort but results in clarity while to recollect means the thing remembered is somewhat hazy or possibly altered in memory by the passage of time.

relict – a widow, from the Latin, meaning a living organism surviving from an earlier time.

relish – a small gift, usually considered to be a luxury, as a return for a favor, an example being a small extra added to an order by a merchant as a thank you to a favored customer such as a flower given to the purchaser's wife or an extra roll or a sweet included for free with a customer's order.

repairing lease – to be on a repairing lease means the person has left town and fled to the country to escape creditors because he's broke and unable to raise any more money.

reprobate – an unprincipled, wicked or depraved person; a scoundrel. This can also be an adjective as in reprobate behavior or conduct.

retiring room – for ladies to retreat to, like a ladies room at a ball or a theatre with maids to mend torn gowns or fix one's hair as well providing toilet facilities.

ring a peal (over someone) – yell at them; scold them; give them hell.

River Tick - to be on the River Tick or up the River Tick was to be totally broke; to be without funds and living on credit.

rolled up – totally out of funds; broke.

roguish – knavish; rascally; playfully mischievous.

rookery – (in London and other large cities) a crowded, dirty, and poor tenement house or group of such houses. What we would call a slum.

Rotten Row – from a corruption of the French phrase "route de roi" meaning king's row. It was used by the upper classes as a path for horseback riding and located in the southern section of Hyde Park in London.

round as a bait pot – fat and roly-poly.

rout – a large, formal evening party or social gathering of the upper classes.

Royal Academy of Arts – founded by important artists of the day in 1768, it ran a school for young artists. It also served as a public art gallery when those did not exist anywhere else in England though it did charge a fee for viewing its shows. During the Regency, the academy was located in Somerset House. There was also a juried Summer Exhibition each year from May to August which helped artists to become known to the public and to sell their art.

Royal Amphitheatre – Originally designed to hold equestrian exhibitions. In addition, it had a huge stage where military shows with soldiers, cannon and horses could be staged. It also had a circus ring and so is a forerunner of the circus as we know it for it presented acts such as jugglers, clowns, and tightrope walkers. It was often referred to as Astley's Amphitheatre for its founder but by the Regency was legally the Royal Amphitheatre. It was mostly popular from its founding in 1776 to 1809 when it closed. It reopened in 1812 but struggled until 1826 when it closed for good.

rusticate – go to the country; stay in the country or go to the country such as a person might if too much in debt and trying to escape creditors **or** said of a student who was sent down (suspended) from university as punishment for failure or bad behavior.

S

sapiently – wisely; sagely.

sapskull – numskull, idiot, fool.

sarcenet – a fine and soft fabric, often made of silk and often in a twill weave used for ladies' gowns, especially formal ones.

Sassenach – from the Saxons – the disparaging word used by Scots for the English.

sauce – impertinence; insolence; pertness.

savoir-faire – knowledge of just what to do in any situation; tact; adaptability; adroitness; diplomacy; discernment; skill; ability.

savoir-vivre – knowledge of the world and the ways or usages of polite society.

sawyer (or top sawyer) – a skilled driver of horses.

Season – prime time for social events for high society in London. It began after Easter and lasted through June. A variety of entertainments were held during this period, and many were designed as a way for young ladies to meet potential mates. The social events usually started in March or later if Easter was late.

sennight – a week (see fortnight above).

set one's cap for – to try to catch a particular sweetheart or person as your husband.

shallowpate – another word for fool. Also called a dunderhead.

sharp-set – hungry.

sixes and sevens – to be at sixes and sevens is to be confused and unsettled.

skylark – (see climbing boy above).

sly-boots – one who is able to fool, trick, deceive; crafty, tricky, wily, shifty, deceptive person.

smalls – a term for men's undershorts (which many men did not wear until much later in the Regency).

Smithfield bargain – a seeming bargain but where the purchaser is taken advantage of or cheated. It is also used to describe marriages contracted solely for financial gain, implying the woman is being bought and sold like cattle in the Smithfield Market in London.

snuff – powdered tobacco that one carried in a small box and put into one's nose causing a person to sneeze. For most of the Regency, this was only an older person's habit dating from the 1700's.

sobriquet – nickname or special name a person is called or known as.

soiree – an evening party or social gathering, especially one held for a particular purpose such as a musical recital.

solicitor – a lawyer who deals in contracts and wills but does not argue in a court of law (see barrister above).

sovereign – the ruler of the nation **or** a gold coin of England worth one pound that in 1813 replaced the guinea coin which had been worth one pound and one shilling (see guinea above).

Spanish coin – false flattery that is unwanted.

special license – a license issued by the Archbishop of Canterbury or his office in Doctor's Commons, or by an archbishop in some cases. For a fee, it would allow a couple to marry at any time and place without banns being read. It could also take place anywhere, not just in a chapel and not just between 8 am and noon as a wedding based on banns had to. This then could be a private wedding. The license for this and the time limit for a wedding based on banns were both good for three months. Since the cost was high, this was an option only for the wealthy and those with the right connections such as members of the ton (see banns above).

spectacles – eye glasses. These had been invented in the 1700s but were considered ugly (rightly so in most cases for the way they were made) and so were rarely worn in public. If help seeing was needed, most upper class people used a quizzing class instead (see quizzing glass above). Poor people couldn't afford anything.

spencer – a short jacket for women to be worn over a dress. It came down to the high waist of Regency gowns and so the bottom edge was just under the breasts.

spillikins – the game of jackstraws or pick-up-sticks.

spy-glass – (also called a glass or a telescope). Spy-glass could also be used to mean an opera glass or an eye glass.

stand up with – to escort a woman to a ball, soiree, or any other social occasion of importance.

St. Leger – one of the three great horse races of the year during the Regency, it was held at Doncaster (see Derby and Newmarket above).

strait – when used as an adjective, it means narrow, limited, confining or focused.

stays – a short or long corset worn by Regency ladies but more usually short for most of the Regency. This was much lighter and shorter than that which women wore later in the Victorian period.

stillroom – a room in a large house where herbs and flowers were distilled into what we would call essential oils and also dried to be used to make many products the household might need. They were used to make medicines such as tinctures (medicines dissolved in alcohol), ointments, pills, cosmetics items such as rose and lavender waters, and cleaning products such as scented beeswax for polishing furniture. Dried herbs were used for herbal teas to help with such problems as morning sickness or to help someone sleep. Herbs were also dried to flavor food or drinks or to put in sachets to keep moths out of woolen items.

From medieval times into the Regency, this room was the domain of the lady of the house with servants to help where necessary. She also taught her daughters the skills needed so that they could also carry out these same skills when they married and had their own households. As society moved toward the Victorian, these chores became the housekeeper's and/or cooks' domain since many of the products produced in the stillroom were now available commercially and did not need to be produced at home. Then the room was used to make jams and jellies as well as home-made drinks and for storing perishables such as baked goods.

surety – a guarantee to someone of security against loss or damage or for the fulfillment of some obligation, the payment of debt, etc. or a pledge, guarantee or bond of a person who has made himself responsible for another especially as a bondsman for another person's behavior or actions.

swell – in English slang - a fashionable man; in American slang of the time, a man with new money.

T

tabby – an old maid; a spinster, probably from the idea that old, single women kept cats for company as a cat is often called a tabby.

take – a young lady who did not "take" during her Season did not win any admirers or suitors. To not take was a social tragedy or disgrace.

tangled in the gob – Cockney term for difficulty in speaking.

tangled in the nob – Cockney term for being highly confused or insane.

taproom – the bar room of an inn or hotel.

taradiddle – falsehood or lie.

Tattersall's – the most prestigious horse market and horse auction in Regency London.

tell-tale – one who gossips; a tattletale.

Theatre Royal, Drury Lane – This was the oldest theatre existing in Regency London. It burned down in 1809 and didn't reopen until 1812. The owner went bankrupt in 1826, and it then passed through many owners, but it still exists today as a theatre. It also was one of two theatres in the Regency to be allowed to put on legitimate theatre, that is plays with dialogue but without music. (See Covent Garden Theatre above.)

tendre – feeling of love; attraction; fondness.

ticket porter – a porter (carrier of bags) who is licensed and wears a badge to show he is licensed by the train company and thus not a thief. Mainly connected with trains in the later

Regency.

tiger – a liveried groom who rode on a seat at the back of a gentleman's phaeton or curricle when the gentleman was driving himself. He is usually small and often, but not always, young. His seat was between the springs of the curricle or phaeton. The later cabriolet had a platform at the rear on which the tiger stood. He also managed the horses when his master ascended to or descended from the seat and sometimes took the reins to exercise the horses while his master temporarily left the vehicle. He could also serve as a go-fer for the gentleman. It was something of a status symbol in some circles to have the smallest possible tiger.

tizz – a tizzy, a dither.

toad-eaten – flattered and made up to. A toad-eater is a sycophant or flatterer; a toady.

toadstool – a derogatory word for a person who has made a fortune but is not highborn. Like toadstools, they were thought off as growing from manure (see mushroom above).

touched (in the upper works) – crazy; insane; not all there.

Town – when town is capitalized in the Regency, it always refers to London.

Town bronze – polish or style reflecting the style of one who lived in London.

town coach – like a landau except it had a hard top and was even more expensive. If owned by nobility, it often had the family's coat of arms on its door (see landau above).

ton – (or sometimes bon ton) - originally a French word meaning manners or breeding, it was used in the Regency to refer to the highest members of society, what we would call the ruling class. It is pronounced like "tone" (see quality or beau monde above).

travail – pain, suffering, anguish, torment.

trenchant – effective; distinct; clear-cut; keen; sharp; cutting.

truculent – fierce, savage or violent; brutally harsh or scathing.

tun – a large cask or barrel for holding liquids; a measure of capacity for liquor equal to 252 gallons.

Turkish bath – a business establishment where a bather entered a steam room, then washed, had a massage and lastly took a cold shower. It was a luxury available only to men.

U

under (or below) the hatches – without funds; in debt.

up the spout – broke.

V

vail – tip or gratuity to servant or such as in "He gave the servant a generous vail."

valet – a male servant who takes care of a man's clothes and gives him personal service such as tying his cravat, giving him skin care if necessary, shaving him and getting him to bed when he is drunk or ill. He also sees that his master's clothes are cleaned and pressed correctly and that he is dressed properly when he goes out.

Vauxhall Gardens – the most famous and expensive pleasure garden of the time, it was located across the Thames from London proper and offered concerts, dancing, spectacles and fireworks displays. However, it also had secluded pavilions one could hire for intimate suppers and dark walks suitable for illicit assignations.

verge – the point at which something begins or happens; the brink or a limiting edge, margin or boundary of something; a border. In modern Britain, it is the piece of land at the edge of a road.

vingt-et-un – this card game is what is now known as blackjack or 21. In fact, its name in French means 21.

vixen – bad-tempered or quarrelsome woman.

vouchers – were required to gain admittance to Almack's. They could only be given out by one of the Patronesses, the women who controlled who could attend and what dances could be allowed. The patronesses were powerful within the ton (see Almack's, patroness, assembly room, and ton above).

vowels – written IOUs given in place of paying a debt and due the person to whom they are given. They were debts of honor and had to be paid before any other debts.

W

waltz – considered somewhat shocking because of the physical contact maintained between partners. Not allowed at Almack's until 1815. When it was allowed there, a young lady required the consent of one of the patronesses of Almack's for her first waltz (see Almack's, patroness and precessed above).

warren – a crowded district or building (see rookery) **or** a piece of ground filled with burrows where rabbits or other small animals live **or** a piece of land enclosed and preserved for hunting small game.

watering pot – person who cries when they shouldn't or cries too often or too easily

waters (taking the waters) – the waters in spa towns like Tunbridge Wells and Bath were thought to have healing powers, so to "take the waters" means either to drink or bathe in these mineral waters.

wear the willow – to mourn the loss of a love or to be lovelorn. It is from the use of the willow tree as a common symbol of mourning due to the way its branches droop toward the ground.

went to the wall – went broke or went for the now rather than the future or supported someone or some cause to the fullest extent.

Weston – a famous Regency tailor of gentlemen's clothes. The jackets were so closely fitted that often a man had trouble getting in or out of them without help.

whist – this card game was similar to modern bridge but only two people played at a time.

White's – founded in 1693 for men in the aristocracy, it is the oldest men's club in England. In the Regency, it was located on St. James Street, as it still is. Again, a man was elected to the club which was favored by the more conservative lords. Most of its members, if not all of them, were members of the Tory party (see Brooks's and Boodle's above).

Widow (the Widow) – In the Regency, this did not just refer to a woman whose husband had died. London clubmen of the time would ask for the Widow and get champagne. Specifically they were asking for a bottle of Veuve Clicquot, the most sought after being the 1811 cuvee which its maker, the French woman, Barbe-Nicole Clicquot Ponsardin, managed to get past the English naval blockades even during the Napoleonic Wars. In fact, when Napoleon abdicated in 1814, the British and Russians in France toasted their victory with the Widow, not knowing that the emperor would stage a short comeback in 1815 leading to the Battle of Waterloo. After the war, that champagne continued to be popular in many countries. The word "clicquot" means widow in French.

wigsby – a wig wearer in this time when it was not fashionable to do so.

windbag – person who talks a great deal but does not say much.

white marriage – one with no sex between the spouses.

Y

yard of tin – the horn, generally a yard long, used by the guard of a mail coach or stage coach to warn of approach and departure at a toll gate or an inn. Mail coaches did not have to stop for toll gates. At an inn, the horn was used to warn that the coach was arriving with possible customers and to have a team of horses ready to be changed as soon as it did arrive and to have the mail bag ready as well. When the coach left the inn, the horn was used to announce its departure.

A REGENCY LEXICON FOR READERS AND WRITERS

ABOUT THE AUTHOR

Carol Jo Goss, an omnivorous reader from an early age, discovered Jane Eyre and Elizabeth Bennett at age ten. Those feisty heroines sparked her lifelong love of romance, the Regency and, of course, England where she lived and taught English literature and history for a year and where she's returned many times.

She now lives on a pond in Michigan with her wonderful husband and champion proofreader as well as her crazy but lovable cats in a house she designed. When she isn't sequestered in her office writing the kinds of books she loves to read, she enjoys gardening, cooking, reading, and researching the Regency. She also loves history, baseball and hockey (Go Red Wings!), and obviously, travel anywhere in the world.

Manufactured by Amazon.ca
Bolton, ON